The Rage in Your Eyes

Alexander Baskakow

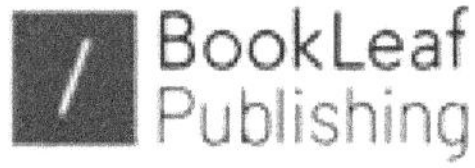
BookLeaf
Publishing

Presentation by *BookLeaf Publishing*

Web: www.bookleafpub.com

E-mail: info@bookleafpub.com

ISBN: 9789357211284

First edition 2022

DEDICATION

To you

(not you, the other one)

Basement

Imprisoned by the shackles
Of a never-ending loneliness
I reach for the phone
But, like always, I just stare at it
The same walls that have surrounded me
Are starting to look bare
Tired, I shut my eyes and writhe
In a self-induced despair
It could be so easy
And I could be so free
But how can I see the world
When I can't face what's in front of me?
A life filled with beauty
Or an eternity of dread
I try to plug my ears but can't stop
The voice that's in my head
They sound so familiar
And yet so distant
Does it even exist
Or have I always dreamt it?

Salesman

I am the stray dog
Sleeping in the thunderstorm
With cold, wet fur

I am the abused son
Of the drunken salesman
Beaten into a pulp
Drink the nectar of my flesh

I am the taste of vomit
On his lips
I make him sick, he says
Fist, kick, fist, bite, cry

I am here
And I don't want to be

Lock the door and pray for death
This I wish with every breath

Bottles

Before you existed,
Happiness was found where the sun shone
bright.
Now it's at the bottom of a bottle.
I guess we're one in the same.
We disrupt the lives of those we love.
We try our best but it's not enough.
We shovel shit.
We eat ourselves.
I will hold your hand.
Feel my warmth and weep.
I've never felt this way before, you said.
Neither have I.
It hurts, but it hurts so good.

Tired

Tired of the endless one-sided conversations,
of the selfishness and ignorance,
of the spiteful words and false accusations,
of the glazed over look in the distance,
of the walls you built that I can't knock down,
of the silence and the apathy,
of the things you do when I'm not around,
of the self-induced mental agony.

Tired of you being tired of me,
I think I'll go to sleep.
Tired of you being tired of me,
My only friend the sheep.

Branch

I will carve my words
Into the side of the tree
With the sturdy branch

I will take my time
Have a seat and look around
On the sturdy branch

I will make my peace
With the people of the world
From the sturdy branch

I will tie the rope
And in my final moments
Thank the sturdy branch

Guts

Sitting
Staring
The page is blank
I thought you knew yourself
You know everything
Spill your guts
Out onto the floor
Show the world
This is what you wanted
Isn't it?
Are you a coward
Or a liar?
Face the truth
This isn't for YOU
It's for THEM
And they don't seem to care

Cassandra

It's like talking with a mouth full of razorblades.

Every word hurts.
Every word cuts deeper and deeper.

I don't want to have to say these things to you.

Cassandra, I am. Cassandra, I am.

Even though you won't want to,
You'll see my words are true.

Every wish.
Every desire.
Every hope for a season together.

All gone, all gone, all gone.

Cassandra, I am. Cassandra, forever.

Nothing feels worse.
My pathetic verse.

Animal

Like an animal
You lead me to a post
And tie me
Beat me
Whip me
Sever my tongue
So that I may not speak
But only scream
Like an animal
For that is what I am

Goodbye Sky

When the sky comes crashing down,
I will look up with a smile on my face.

It's the end of the world.

It's everything I ever wanted.

Punching Bag

It's every eye staring at me
It's trying to find the words
To describe myself
In a way that won't make me seem so vile
To the rest of the insipid population

I guess we go hand in hand in a way
Life needs a punching bag
Life needs a stepping stone
I exist to fulfill a consumer need
The need to patronize

I could feel the sun
But my presence must not be known
I will fly by night
Into the hearts of imaginary creatures
They come in my dreams
They come as friends
Along with my hands
They are all that I've got

So I will continue to push away
Those who claim to love
And those who are blind to me
I wouldn't want to have it any other way

Bliss

Lay my body out to sea
For this is where I want to be
Sat beside the sinking ship
That once set sail inside of me

Lay me in the cold abyss
The waters touch my final kiss
And as my body slowly sinks
Blind my eyes and bathe in bliss

Noticed

I wore a new cologne today
It had notes of cedar and bergamot
And cost half my paycheck

But you didn't notice

I cut my hair today
You always said you liked it short
I even told the hairdresser about you

But you didn't notice

I tried a new recipe today
I got to try out that new knife I bought
It looked delicious so I sent you a picture

But you didn't notice

I wrote you a letter
Saying all the things I never could
And never even thought I would

But you didn't notice

I drove up to your house today

My new knife in hand
Cut myself on your doorstep
And knocked three times

I wanted to make absolutely sure
That you would see

The look of horror on your face
Tells me that you did

Finally

You noticed me

Frankie

Three Stooges and Little Rascals re-runs
Hosted by that child actor fuck
Are the only things
That keep my personal parental figure
From suddenly remembering
That they have yet to use
Their new claw hammer
They got for Christmas

The walls of the house are too old
The shed outside is too cold

Let's see how these nails
Fit into the palm your hand boy
Where are your friends now boy
Where are your followers now boy
I need a new change of pants now boy
I'm gonna ride you like a cowboy now boy
You'd like that now wouldn't you boy
Wouldn't you boy

Tears

I take a hit off the cigarette
A habit I very much regret
The house is empty
But the table is set
A cold wind blows
The earth is wet
I turn my gaze outside

In the trees, I can see
The ghost of you searching for me
But still I hide
And let black plumes of smoke
Mask my weary eyes
My face is wet
From the tears I cry

Chamber

Find me in my room
A chamber of self-pity
Hiding from the world

Point at me and laugh
My hideous reflection
Breaks every mirror

Lead me to the edge
I will take my leap of faith
Into a new life

Where nothing exists
And I can finally be
Forever at peace

Drool

You know I can't stand you
You filthy little creature
With a mouth full of drool
And grimy fur
The truest depiction of an animal
That I have ever seen or heard
But now matter how hard I try
To push you away
And ignore your gaze
You lovingly caress my hand
With your cheek
And fall asleep

Agony

Agony is red
Like thousands of knives
Inflicting thousands of wounds
Seeping into an endless stream

Agony is burning
A smoldering flame
That will never be put out
Rendering black all in its path

Agony is inside me
Kicking, clawing, screaming
It wants to be let out
But I will keep it within

Agony exists
And it is here to stay
I close my eyes, hold my breath
And let it swallow me whole

Pilgrim

Specks of dirt and unearthed remains
Dust and coffee grinds and daisy chains
Threaded by our children
Sucked up into the everlasting void
At a pace too quick to comprehend
The wind blows and the trees bend
One solitary pilgrim
Stares up into the everlasting void
Is it their right
To the beg the question "why?"

Purity

For a moment
There was nothing
No sound
No movement
No disorder
A vacant world
Unshackled from life

It was beautiful
There was purity
In the isolation
All we knew
All we had
All we wanted
Was each other

But it was just a moment
Life moved on
And took you with it

Red Glow

A bleeding heart
An object still worth holding onto
Covered in ashes
It is the only thing that remains
I'm still searching
For a light at the end of the tunnel
The only presence is a red glow
Growing ever stronger
I'll hold my face forwards and bear it
This is something I have to do
If I want to move on
I want to move on

Found

I peel away layers
Of skin and flesh and bone
And uncover the soul
Of the being
I've been led to believe
Is myself

An empty void
Blurry and black
Both inviting
And denying
I reach out my hand
And it hides from me

Time stands still
For what seems to be
An eternity
But I have made a vow
I will continue to try
To reclaim my soul

I beckon it with words
And songs and prayers
And stories about myself
Every insignificant little detail

Comes pouring out
In an endless stream of memory

Then suddenly
The black turns to white
And everything makes sense
I've finally found my vessel
A body reborn
To be cherished forever